❀❀ Dedications ❀❀

With love to my grandchildren,
who give my life new meaning and
have set me on this journey.
~ AMC

To my grandson, Brayden Smith.
Live your dreams!
~ LS

Graphic Design & Editing by Nicole Lavoie of www.JustSayingDezigns.com

Thanks to so many who have worked tirelessly to make this book a reality:
My Family, The ILML Community, Ocean State Labradoodles,
Cassandra Bowen of Uzuri Designs, IAPC Members & Mentors,
The Little Labradoodle Advisory, Puppy Pickup Day Beta-Readers,
and the backers of our Kickstarter Campaign

Little Labradoodle Publishing, LLC
www.thelittlelabradoodle.com · info@thelittlelabradoodle.com

Proudly Printed in the United States by
Signature Book Printing · www.sbpbooks.com

Library of Congress Control Number: 2018909551

First Edition: 2018 · ISBN 978-1-7324566-4-8

The Little Labradoodle: Puppy Pickup Day

Written by April M. Cox / Illustrated by Len Smith
Graphic Design & Editing by Just Saying Dezigns

This Little Labradoodle
BOOK BELONGS TO

"Today is the day.
Wake up, wake up!
Today is the day!"
barked the littlest pup.

Seven more puppies
jumped from their beds
as the little one yelled,
"Wake up, sleepy heads!"

Primping and fussing
with hairbrush and comb;
today, all the puppies
will get a new home.

So eager and happy,
they ran off to play,
excited and ready
for their big day!

When two of the doodles
played tug with a rope,
for the littlest pup,
there wasn't much hope.

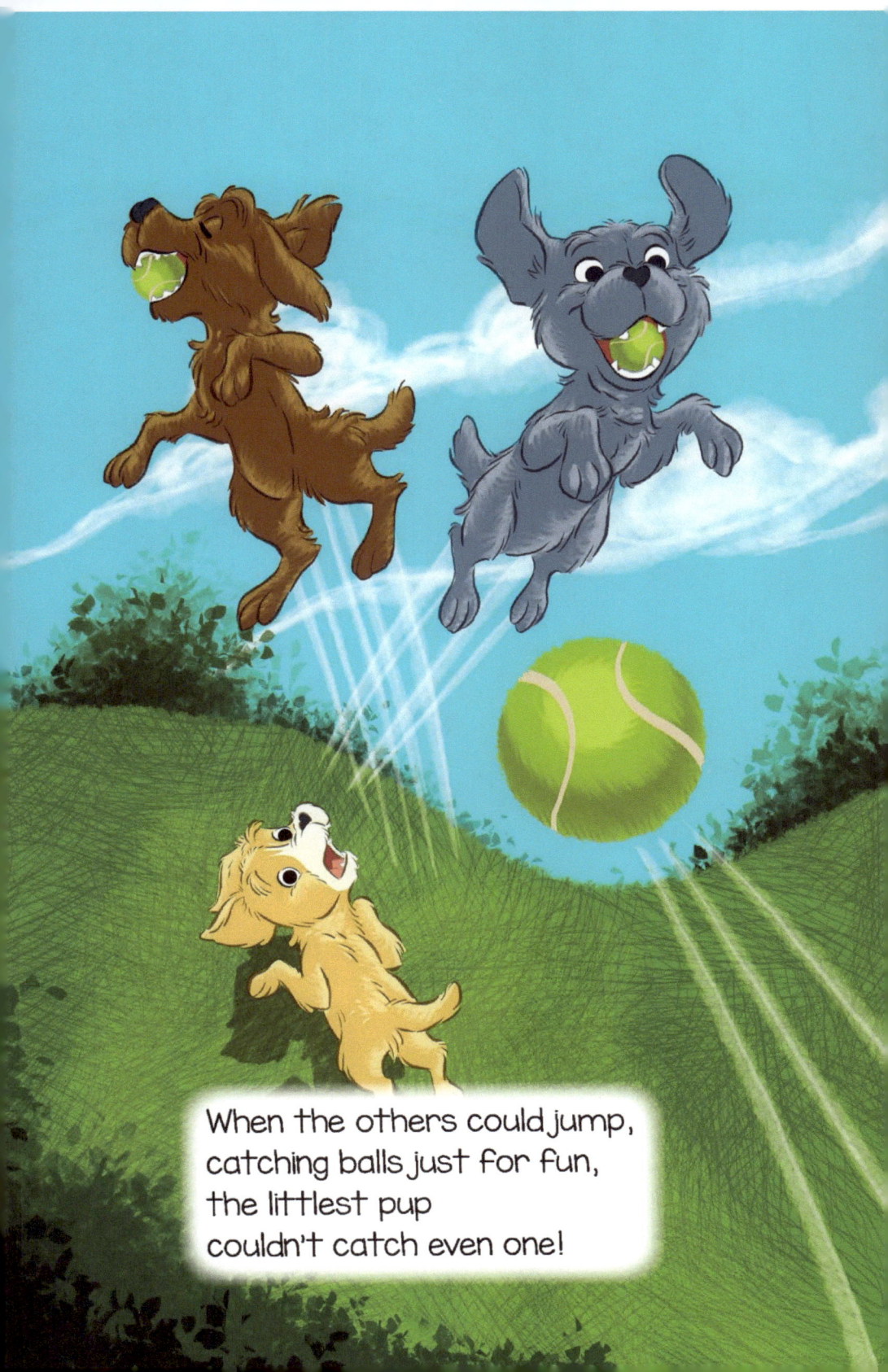

When the others could jump,
catching balls just for fun,
the littlest pup
couldn't catch even one!

"You're too small!"
the other doodles cried,
as with a big thump,
he fell off the slide.

He sighed, and he plopped himself
under a tree,
saw rabbits and said,
"Hey, you're little like me!"

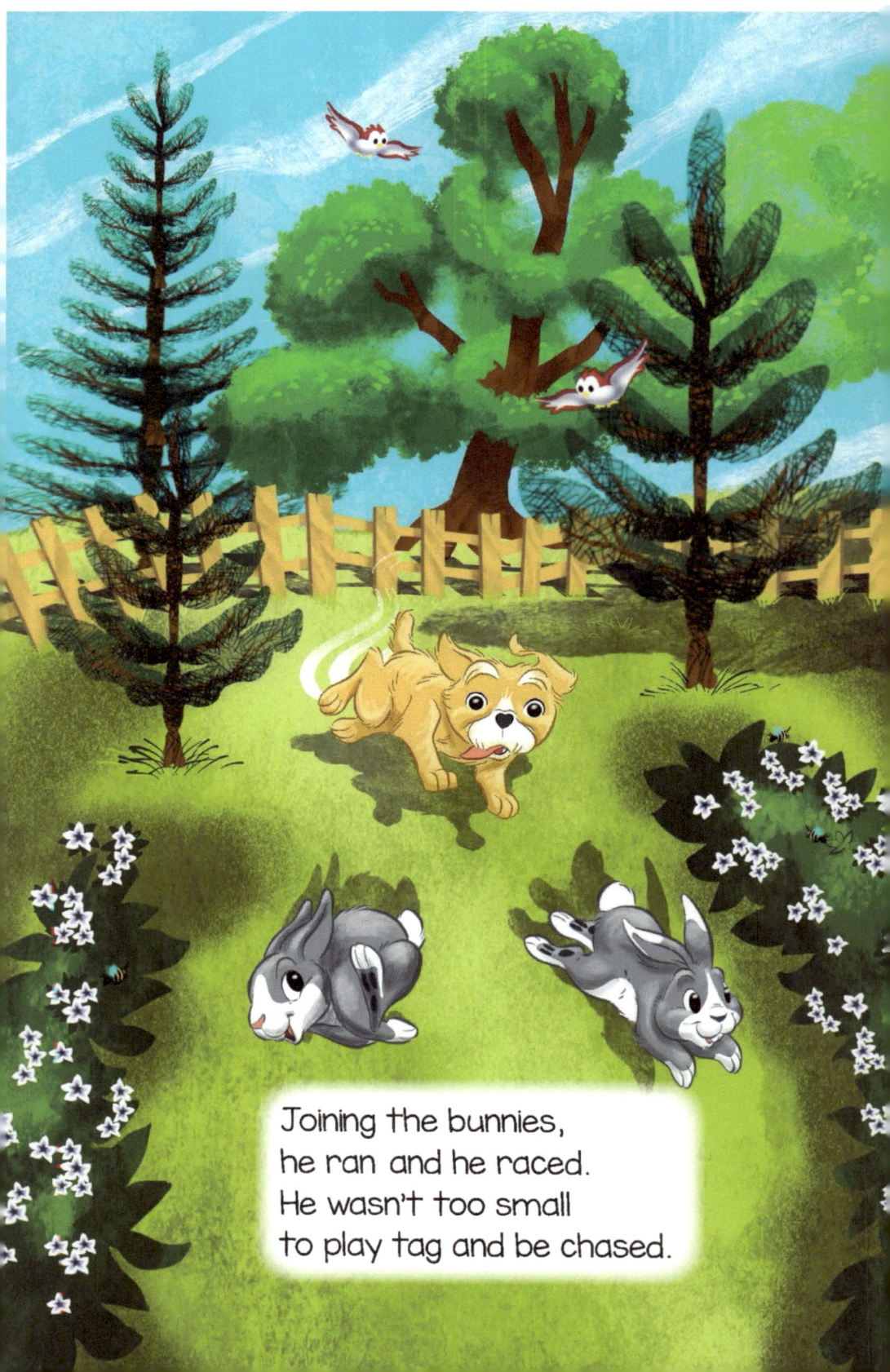

Joining the bunnies,
he ran and he raced.
He wasn't too small
to play tag and be chased.

Under bushes and trees,
over bridges they crossed;
then little pup yelped,
"Oh no, I am lost!"

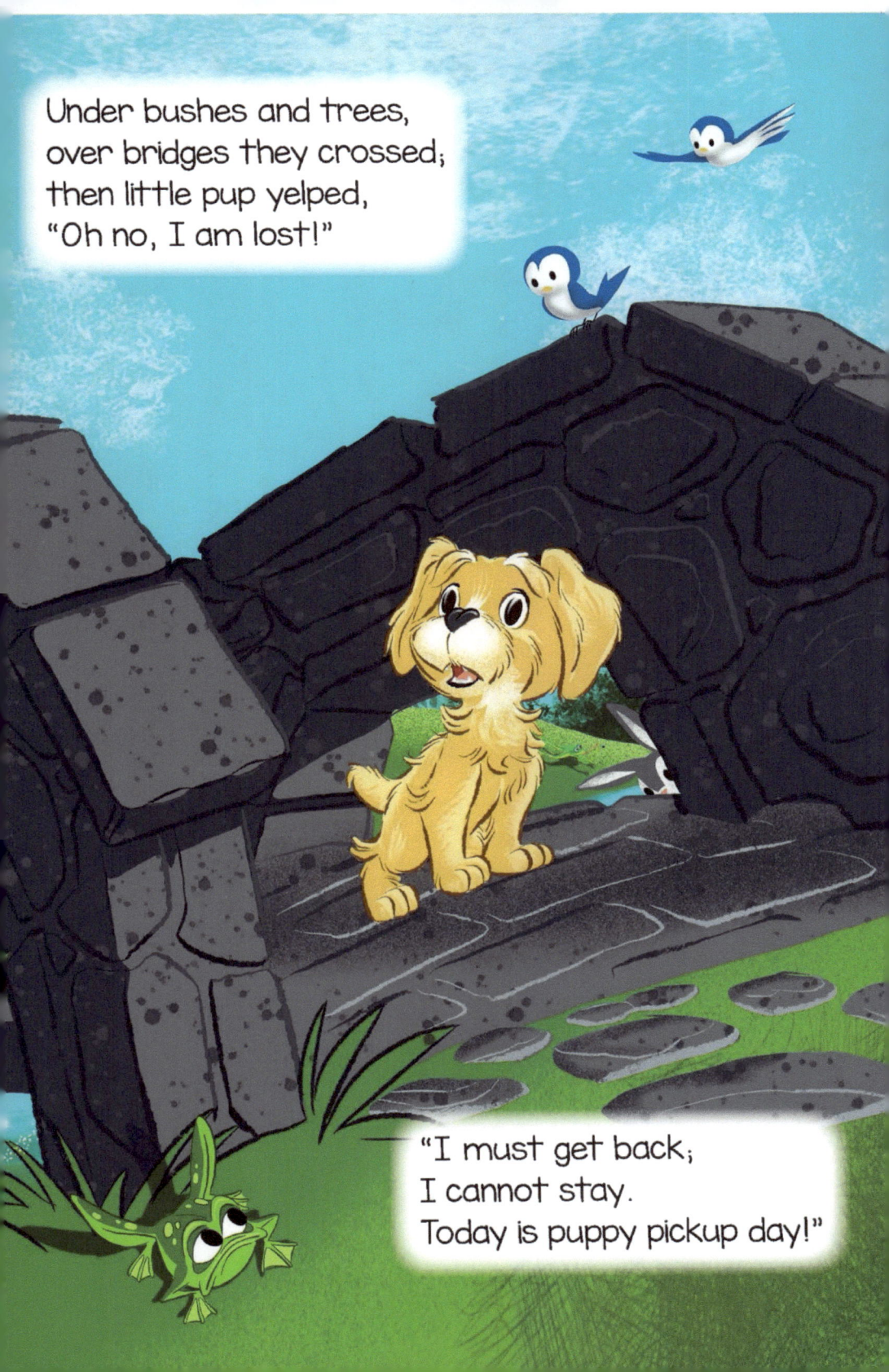

"I must get back;
I cannot stay.
Today is puppy pickup day!"

In the meantime,
some families began to arrive.
They each picked up doodles,
and then there were five.

Aunt Nola Doodle
said goodbye to each one,
as she patted their heads
a few times just for fun.

"Hello!", said the puppy
to Eevee, the cat.
"I have run a long way.
How do I get back?"

"Through the tall grass,"
she said, "over the hill;
find a small stream
and a bullfrog named Bill."

He walked by the water
looking for Bill,
who was chasing a fly
and wouldn't stand still.

"I must get back; I cannot stay.
Today is puppy pickup day!"

While the pup was wondering
what he should do,
three more were picked up,
and then there were two.

With grandkids excited,
who just couldn't wait,
we drove to meet up
with our fluffy playmate.

Grandpa and Kairi
were singing a song,
with Jackson and
me clapping along.

The pup saw his friend, Abra,
as she came into sight,
and he knew everything
would soon be alright.

"I must get back; I cannot stay.
Today is puppy pickup day!"

They then heard giggles
from kittens at play.

"Join us," they all said.
"It's a beautiful day!"

"I must get back; I cannot stay,
Today is puppy pickup day!"

"Follow us to a shortcut,"
the pup's new friends said.

He tried to hold tight,
but fell right on his head!

The littlest doodle
ran back toward the gate.
He squeezed under the fence,
afraid he was late.

"I must get back; I cannot stay.
Today is puppy pickup day!"

After a long and bumpy drive,
his very own family
was last to arrive.

Could this new family
love a clumsy pup,
whose legs had trouble
keeping up...

Who needed help
after too many falls,
failed at tug
and couldn't catch balls?

He worried his family
wouldn't like him at all,
but he gave them a smile
and tried to stand tall.

He was dirty and scared
and just wanted to hide,
but he took a deep breath,
and he headed outside.

Then Bella saw him,
"Look, here he is!
Have you ever seen a face
sweeter than his?"

"All dirty," said Kairi,
making a face,
but Nola knew how
to remove every trace.

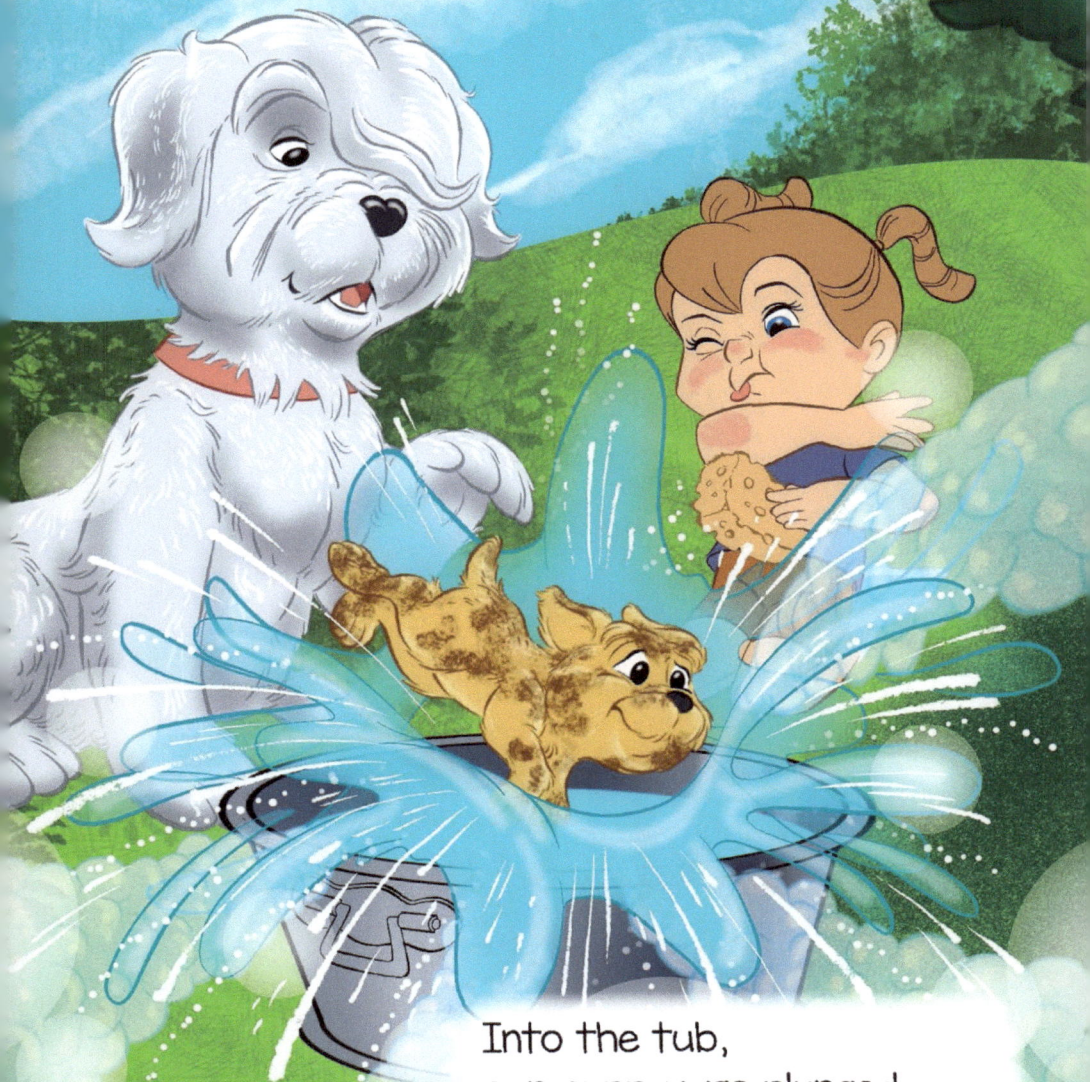

Into the tub,
our puppy was plunged.
Off came the grass
and the mud with a sponge.

As the dirt and the grime
were then washed from his eyes,
he CLEARLY saw now
that they loved his small size.

Puppy pickup day at last was done.
With a final pat from Nola,
"Make us proud, little one!"

"Welcome to the family.
It's been quite a day.
The first of many adventures
coming your way!"

Look for more adventures with
Brady, The Little Labradoodle,
and his friends coming soon!

Visit our website and join our mailing list at
www.thelittlelabradoodle.com

Be sure to also check out...
The Little Labradoodle: Puppy Pickup Day
- Companion Coloring Book
- Lesson Plan
- Little Labradoodle Plush
- eBook
- Audio Book

Coming SOON in The Little Labradoodle Series:
- The Little Labradoodle: The Big Move
- The Little Labradoodle: New Baby
- The Little Labradoodle: Bullies Beware
- The Little Labradoodle: Puppy Kindergarten

Check out these other great titles from
Little Labradoodle Publishing:
- Little Labradoodle & Friends:
  Coloring & Activity Book
- Doodle Lovers Adult Coloring Book

Follow us on social media at...
TheLittleLabradoodle
@TheLittleLabradoodle
lil_labradoodle

About the Illustrator

Len Smith has spent his entire career in children's entertainment, from Hanna-Barbera studio to Disney Feature and TV animation to Mattel Toys.

Len designed Toontown in the film "Who Framed Roger Rabbit" and designed the main characters for the Disney Afternoon series "Talespin" and "Bonkers".

He also worked on the four-time Emmy winning series "The New Adventures of Winnie the Pooh" and was very proud to do the illustration for "The Little Labradoodle: Puppy Pickup Day".

About the Author

April M. Cox, an Author and Entrepreneur who has always enjoyed creative writing, rediscovered children's picture books while reading to her grandchildren. Her little labradoodle often sat with them and was the inspiration for this book series.

Little Labradoodle Publishing was founded in 2018 with a passion to publish beautifully illustrated books that children would love and parents would appreciate. Little Labradoodle books provides underlying themes like gratitude, kindness, friendship, diversity, self-acceptance and inclusion.

www.ingramcontent.com/pod-product-compliance
Lightning Source LLC
Chambersburg PA
CBHW040748150426
42811CB00059B/1512